SELF-HELP
for the
HELPLESS

SHELLEY WILSON

To Ladey,
Thank you for your
support and our chats!
With love Shelley Wilson
xxx

bhc
press™

Livonia, Michigan

Editor: Joni Firestone
Proofreader: Jamie Rich

SELF-HELP FOR THE HELPLESS
Copyright © 2021 Shelley Wilson

Published by BHC Press

Library of Congress Control Number: 2020936636

ISBN: 978-1-64397-173-5 (Softcover)
ISBN: 978-1-64397-174-2 (Ebook)

For information, write:
BHC Press
885 Penniman #5505
Plymouth, MI 48170

Visit the publisher:
www.bhcpress.com

BOOKS BY SHELLEY WILSON

How I Changed My Life in a Year!

How I Motivated Myself to Succeed

Meditation for Children

Motivate Me! An Oracle Guidebook

TABLE OF CONTENTS

For anyone who has ever felt helpless—I believe in you.

SELF-HELP
for the
HELPLESS

INTRODUCTION

For many years I was clueless when it came to self-help. The phrase hadn't entered my orbit yet. My life revolved around school then college, my friends and family, and going out and having as much fun as I could. I had no responsibilities except myself—and I often wonder how I managed that!

Taking care of my emotional needs, my mental health, and my inner child never crossed my mind back then. Why would it?

Unfortunately, it often takes a cataclysmic life event for us to realise that looking after our needs is vital to our well-being and survival. Redundancy, bereavement, domestic abuse, illegal substance abuse, divorce, health issues, alcoholism, and other life changes impact us on several levels.

Someone dealing with an abusive relationship copes with the same emotional upheaval as another person who has been made redundant. Rock bottom is rock bottom no matter the circumstances surrounding it.

Those changes create a ripple effect within us, and we begin to look at life differently. We question everything, and we trust none of the answers we receive.

It often feels lonely to navigate the waters of despair and with these turbulent emotions comes the additional threat of depression and anxiety. How do you cope with a life-changing event or situation when your mental state is also affected? The black fog of depression is merciless and adds to feelings of isolation, misery, and anxiety.

I still remember the first time I stepped into the Mind, Body, Spirit section at my local bookshop. I'd just walked out of my seven-year marriage with my three young children in tow, who were two, three, and five years old. My life had crumbled around me, and I felt lost, lonely, and terrified about the future. Standing in that bookshop, I looked at the sea of book spines claiming to fix everything wrong in my life, and I panicked. When had it gone so wrong? Why was I so broken? Where did it all fall apart? Why wasn't I walking to the fantasy section where I felt safe?

Just as I was about to give up and walk away, a single book caught my eye—*The Secret* by Rhonda Byrne. I'd never heard about it and wasn't familiar with the author, but that title resonated with something deep inside me. "Secret"—my entire life had been a secret. I'd left my friends and extended family behind in Leeds, West Yorkshire when I was eight years old to move to another county with my parents and brother, but being so young I kept my feelings of loss to myself as I didn't fully understand them. Drink, parties, and tearaway moments made up the majority of my teen years, and I hid *all* of that from my parents as many teenagers do. Married life was sullied by domestic violence and emotional abuse, and I never uttered a word until the bitter end when I realised my life, and that of my three children, was in danger. I'd fallen for a man with a

4

turbulent past and his own mental health issues, which I also kept to myself—nobody needed to know how bad I was at relationships—and later on, nobody needed to know I'd failed so miserably at marriage.

Secret after secret after secret.

So, I bought my first self-help book, and my life slowly began to shift.

I'm not saying that by reading one book I was able to fix myself, become a guru in the art of authentic living, and live out my days on a mountaintop in a floaty kaftan and sensible sandals. However, beginning to understand who I was, why I allowed repeating cycles to remain in my life, and what I wanted to do going forward were all essential aspects of dipping my toe into the world of self-help and helped empower me to become who I am today.

Does the term "self-help" only enter our vocabulary when we need it? I believe there's some truth to that, especially if we are also searching for enlightenment. I have always been an avid reader, and yet the Mind, Body, Spirit genre was brand-new to me, like discovering an entire world at the back of a wardrobe. I'd ventured into other nonfiction areas such as craft, cookery, art, and travel, but the "hippie stuff" never resonated until it was exactly what I needed in my life.

If you're at the stage where you're beginning to become more self-aware, then I hope this gentle meander into self-help will give you the tools, knowledge, and strength to try out a few therapies and personal development techniques and leave behind any feelings of helplessness when it comes to being your authentic self. I've included plenty of exercises for you to try as you begin to uncover who you are, what you want, and how you're going to get the life you desire and deserve.

My journey into self-help began over twenty years ago and is ever-evolving as I learn more, understand myself better, and handle the natural changes in my life. You may feel helpless at times, but that's perfectly normal. We often fail to trust our instincts, second-guess our decisions, and revert to a default setting that our parents or teachers or spiritual leaders hammered into us as infants. Over time you'll begin to believe in yourself. You've got this!

WHAT THE HELL DOES SELF-HELP MEAN ANYWAY?

My friend is a talented life coach and strategist as well as a motivational speaker. We have spoken at the same empowering women's events on a few occasions, and I love listening to her straightforward approach to self-help, especially when she starts her talk with: 'It's not all about bubble baths and duvet days!'

Before I began my serious self-work and explored my personal development, I believed what I'd read in countless magazine articles that a bubble bath was the answer. The problem I had was my inability to stay still for an extended period. The idea appealed to me. I used the very best lotions and potions I could find, lit candles, and locked the bathroom door so the kids couldn't disturb me, and then I'd sink below the bubbles and wait. Was I expecting enlightenment? Did I think the water would rinse away my destructive thoughts? Probably. After five minutes, I would leap from the bubbles, pulling the plug, while muttering under my breath that I'd wasted my time on fluffy nonsense. My daughter, on the other hand, can spend an hour or more in the bath and float out of the bathroom like

Cleopatra emerging from her pool of milk. What works for one person doesn't necessarily work for another.

So, if self-help isn't defined by a bubble bath, what the hell is it?

The dictionary explains it as 'the use of one's own efforts and resources to achieve things without relying on others.'

Interesting. Let's stop and think about that for a moment.

The use of one's own = SELF.

Efforts and resources = HELP.

When was the last time you used your own tenacity to get something done? What have you used (resources) to complete a project without asking for help? When you look at it this way, you probably fill your days with self-help elements that you never realised.

Labels can be helpful in some circumstances. We all understand that mental health awareness is a positive label that allows us to explore our mental health, voice any concerns, and share our stories in a safe and supportive community. The self-help label, however, has been reshaped over time by well-meaning therapists, writers, and bloggers to become a thing we must work hard to attain. That's not the case.

The ability to use our efforts to succeed in a task is within us every minute of every day. We need to know how to tap into it, and I think this is where we misunderstand the term and confuse it with self-care.

Let's look at what the dictionary says about self-care: 'the practice of taking action to preserve or improve one's own health.'

There are many similarities between self-help and self-care, but there is also a clear distinction. The therapists I spoke of earlier would benefit significantly from promoting self-care in their business ventures. They aim to help clients achieve balance and optimum well-being for the good of their physical and mental health. However, to run a successful therapy business, many also don't encourage their clients to be self-reliant or use their own efforts and resources to achieve results. Instead, they want their clients to abandon self-help and turn to them for some self-care.

It's interesting to note that the self-help industry is worth over $38 billion a year worldwide. This includes books, workshops, webinars, personal and professional coaching, and motivational speakers.

It isn't just us girls that are searching for answers either. Although there is a need to embrace and celebrate the Me Too movement, young men (my two sons included) are now searching for guidance on how to navigate their lives, conversations, and careers to conform with the revelations brought about by Me Too. Authors like Russell Brand and Matt Haig are helping to reassure male readers that someone understands them, can resonate with the issues facing their mental and physical health, and relate to their worries. Our sons, husbands, brothers, fathers, and colleagues need to know that someone is listening to their concerns too. Being open about mental health is vital to all of us, male and female alike, especially with suicide rates not declining. Self-help or helping ourselves and recognising how and when to help vulnerable people in our community has never been more critical.

What we need to realise from the booming well-being industry is that there are no quick fixes when it comes to self-help. We all buy into the hope that one podcast, book, or workshop will give us the answers we crave, but while these resources can be useful, they will never make us whole.

My bookshelves are crammed full of self-help and personal development titles. I started with *The Secret* and never stopped. Have I found all the answers? No, which is why I keep buying and reading more Mind, Body, Spirit books. My favourite authors change over time as my personal growth evolves. The lessons that Louise Hay and Gabrielle Bernstein taught me ten years ago might not be what Ruby Wax and Viv Groskop can show me today.

In my opinion, we all deserve some positive psychology. There's nothing wrong with looking for answers and trying to unlock ourselves from blockages. Striving for positive well-being needs to be a priority, and it's one that the self-help industry is feeding. Where we do get it wrong as readers is buying books, attending workshops and seminars, listening to talks, but never implementing the points raised. That's why the industry is booming—because we are all searching for a quick fix. Let me tell you right now, there's no such thing. If you want to make any changes to your life then it's going to take time, research, action steps, self-evolvement, and dedication. Buy all the books you need but make a pact with yourself that you'll at least try to action the points each author is making. Only then will you be able to make substantial, focused changes and live a more authentic life.

In its purest form, self-help is a process of change. We are looking to change elements of our life using our own efforts and resources. The myriad of self-help products and services available to us can confuse the process and make us think it's more complicated than it is.

Let me ask you a question: What do you want to change? Let's think about this in terms of you and your life, because if we start to contemplate the state of the world today, we might spiral into a pit of despair that no amount of self-help will fix! Think about your life holistically (as a whole) and work out if there's one area that needs work. Perhaps it's your health, fitness, finances, or relationships. Maybe you want to work on your networking, faith, loyalty, or fun.

You might have several areas that need attention, but I'd always advise you to tackle one at a time.

Once you know what you want to work on, you can begin to put together a strategy to help make the necessary changes. Call them action steps if you like.

The final stage of the self-help process is to ensure you are 100 percent focused and dedicated to making that change.

Yes, there's much more to it than that, of course there is. If self-help was so easy then the industry wouldn't exist at all. We must work incredibly hard to make sure we stay on track—remember, there are no quick fixes. The uplifting thing to bear in mind is that behind all the books, podcasts, seminars, and therapies is an army of people whose goal in life is to help YOU.

I stumbled into writing self-help books by accident. At that stage, I was an avid reader of the Mind, Body, Spirit genre and had amassed many books on a wide range of topics. Each book gave me another piece to the puzzle that was my life. I would read the incredible self-help authors and feel inspired and uplifted by their words or motivated by their stories.

When I began a blog challenge that shared the highs and lows of my fifty-two New Year's resolutions (a different task for every week of the year), I would never have dreamed of seeing myself in the same category as Rhonda Byrne and Susan Jeffers. However, when my first nonfiction book was published (*How I Changed My Life in a Year*), I sat side by side on the bestseller listings with the authors I admired so much.

How did I become a self-help author?

Firstly, I addressed the changes I wanted to make in my life—predominantly I wanted to write a book.

Secondly, I put together a strategy to help make the necessary changes so I could achieve what I wanted. I began blogging weekly on a public platform to keep myself accountable. My writing improved the more I practiced, and the feedback I received from across the globe gave me the incentive to keep going. This, in turn, motivated me to remain focused on the end goal, which was to complete the year of challenges.

One of the resolutions I took part in was NaNoWriMo (National Novel Writing Month) where a fifty-thousand-word novel is written in thirty days. It was during this challenge that I wrote my first young adult fiction novel, *Guardians of the Dead*. After completing the manuscript and going through the rigorous editing process, I published that book and also published *How I Changed My Life in a Year* the same year. And I became a bestselling author!

I'd used my own efforts and resources to achieve the one thing I desired above all else (to become an author) without relying on others—I self-helped myself!

By reading the books the self-help gurus wrote, I'd gathered many tips and tools about personal development, goal setting, and fighting fear, and I'd pooled so many resources to use in my life while taking decisive action that enabled me to realise my biggest dream.

Anyone can do this. YOU can do this.

The reason for writing this book was to show you how a busy, working single mum with wobbly bits and bad dress sense can turn her life around and become her most authentic self. The big names in self-help started somewhere, and by taking away the idea that they have all the answers, it frees us up to explore our needs, embrace our ability to help ourselves, and learn the art of self-care, self-awareness, and self-improvement.

If you're feeling a little bit lost, overwhelmed, anxious, or confused about where you fit in your world, then I hope this book will help you piece together the jigsaw of your own life, and understand better what you need to survive and thrive.

CORE VALUES

A ttending events and workshops on the theme of self-help and personal development is the highlight of my year as I always come away with a pile of notes and a bunch of new friendships. Events like these draw like-minded people together, and there's something powerful about that.

I attended a workshop in Warwickshire some years ago run by the Socially Shared Business Support Network, which runs networking sessions and events for ladies in their local area. One of the speakers was career coach, consultant, and trainer Stephanie Rix, who encourages women to meet their full potential with her workshops and consultancy.

One of the tasks Stephanie set us was to work out what our core values were. If you're not familiar with the term "core values," they are guiding principles that can help you choose between right and wrong and determine which life or career path would be the most fulfilling for you. Living by your values creates a better life balance, but when you work against them, it can have a detrimental effect on your mental health, emotional well-being, and even your physical health. They are unique to you. Your core values may differ significantly from those of your partner, children, friends, or colleagues, and that's normal. Think of your values as a personal code of conduct.

Some of us know instinctively what our values are, but others haven't been able to figure out what is essential in life. In this case it's far too easy to compare yourself to others and focus on what you think you *should* do (you'll find an entire section dedicated to the use of the word *should* later). We become influenced by social media and television and assume our values *should* match that of our favourite celebrity.

Going on instinct, I sorted through the vast array of cards that Stephanie had spread across the table, each one with a single core value written on it. Instead of choosing what I thought I *should*, I drew on the values that spoke to my inner child.

Acceptance
Freedom
Creativity

Let's explore each one for a moment and put them into the context of my life to give you a better idea of why core values are so important.

Acceptance derives from a need to be liked, loved, and approved of. It's something that matters to me for some profound, dark reason. When I write and publish my books, I go through emotional turmoil every time I celebrate a book launch—will people like what I've written? Will it be well received by my peers? Will people think I'm a fraud? And so on, and on. Imposter syndrome is alive and kicking in my head. If I dig a bit deeper, I might begin to realise that moving away from my family and friends at such a young age and having to build relationships from scratch has left me with a feeling of loss and low self-worth. The eight-year-old me walking into that classroom on my first day in a new town was screaming in my head 'What if they don't like me?' Surviving a violent marriage where my husband told me daily how useless, stupid, and pathetic he thought I was weighed me down with low self-esteem and knocked my confidence. All of this impacted my mental health and had a knock-on effect on my values.

Acceptance became a core value because I'd created a limiting belief around the same theme. The more I delve into my history and mind chatter, the more I understand that I only need to accept myself. Nothing more, nothing less. If I can accept who I am, and who I want to be, without the constant squawking of the poisoned parrot chattering inside my head, then this is a strong core value to have.

A quick note on limiting beliefs: They are something that can severely restrict you in some way. Just by believing them, we can make them true. For example, if a teacher told you that your spelling was poor over and over instead of working with you in a more supportive manner, you might develop a limiting belief about not being good at writing, which could restrict a future career and/or self-identity.

When I tell people that **freedom** is one of my core values, it's met with a mix of approval and confusion. I attract friends who relish the ability to travel at the drop of a hat, work from anywhere in the world, and roam the land filling their creative well. Those friends who thrive on structure and order find this strange, especially when they see I'm a single mum of three (I touch on mum guilt later). Both opinions are valid for both types of friends, but for me, freedom represents more than just packing a bag and heading off to the seaside whenever I want. Freedom celebrates that younger version of myself who walked out of a violent marriage. She found freedom by leaping into the unknown: freedom to think for herself, freedom to come and go as she pleased without the fear of upsetting someone.

It's important to me that I don't lose that value. Accepting myself, flaws and all, and being free to choose who I spend my time with, what I do, and why I do it are vital to my well-being.

I chose **creativity** as my last core value. I've always been an arts and crafts kind of girl. Writing has been a massive part of my life since I was old enough to hold a crayon. If you cut me I bleed ink instead of blood. Creativity includes everything I'm passionate about. Writing my books, blogging, running my workshops, creating eCourses and online content, working with my writing clients, journaling, working through my adult colouring books, watching movies…the list goes on. I'm at my happiest with a pen in my hand or when my fingers are flying over a keyboard.

Acceptance. Freedom. Creativity. Three simple words that mean so much. Take a moment to think about your core values and what they mean to you. Write them on a Post-it Note and leave them somewhere visible. Create a graphic on your computer and display them as your screen saver. Living by your core values helps drive your focus and maintain your motivation for life (more on this later).

If you're struggling to think of a core value, here are a few you might want to think about. Why not highlight the ones that jump out at you.

Gratitude	Happiness
Acceptance	Community
Structure	Kindness
Boldness	Love
Contribution	Family
Faith	Responsibility
Growth	Learning
Humour	Adventure
Leadership	Beauty
Pleasure	Honesty
Respect	Fun
Friendship	Peace
Achievement	Reputation
Trust	Stability
Balance	Wisdom
Compassion	Security
Fame	Wealth

Are you drawn to any in particular? Do they resonate with you on a deeper level? You might find more than three, and that's fine. I can relate to about ten of the words above, but Stephanie recommended that we concentrate our efforts on three at a time. Are there values that aren't on the list that you feel a pull toward? You don't have to select your values from a list. It can be useful to play around with them until you discover something that resonates. Our core values may evolve as we grow and our life changes—that's fine too.

To help you figure out your top three core values, try clearing your mind and taking a few deep breaths. No, I'm not going to get all hippie on you, I want you to give this exercise your undivided attention, and not while you're making the dinner, washing the dog, or cutting the grass.

Think about a time when you were frustrated. Why did you feel this way? What happened to make you angry or sad? It's likely that a core value was being suppressed in this situation. Perhaps you'd arranged a night out with the girls and your husband called to say he'd be home late from work, and it messed up your plans. Values of stability, fun, family, or balance might have been tested.

Now think about a wonderful moment in your life. Why were you feeling so happy and content? What happened? In this experience, you will have been respecting your core values. Maybe your husband got home early and told you he'd turned down a client meeting or drinks with his colleagues because he knew you were looking forward to girls' night. Values of loyalty, family, love, and compassion are brought to the forefront.

Finally, I want you to think about what's important to you and your life. In my example, it was creativity, freedom, and acceptance, but what is it for *you*? Do you crave a healthy lifestyle? Perhaps you long to live by the sea and get involved in a small community? Is there a need for fun and adventure now you're an empty nester?

Stay focused on those core values that support you on your current life journey, as that is vital to your life. Score them out of ten if it helps you to work out if you're actively living and working with your values daily.

I know I need to check in with my acceptance value now and then to make sure I'm authentic around this area of my life. Have I slipped back into comparing myself to others? Do I ask for external validation instead of trusting myself? If I see that these elements have crept back in then I'll score my acceptance value at a two or three. With a little self-awareness and work I can get that back up to a nine or ten.

Look at the core values you've chosen and see what you'd score them. Are you happy with them? If the score is low, how can you work toward raising it?

Understanding core values can be hugely beneficial for your self-improvement. There are a range of wonderful books and courses on core values, so if you want to know more, take time out to tap into wisdom, learning, and growth.

ARE WE REALLY HELPLESS?

I noticed something interesting the more involved I became in reading and understanding the principles of self-help and personal development. Instead of making me feel better and more in control, I began to feel confused by all the conflicting information. One author told me to do this, that, and the other to feel balanced and calm, and yet another author was telling me to do the opposite.

At first, I believed there was something wrong with *me*. I was "doing it wrong" and would never feel normal because I was beyond help.

There are a stack of self-help books on my shelf, which remain untouched, some of them written by my favourite authors. Why? Because I wasn't in the right headspace to hear the messages. Does that sound odd?

When we embark on a voyage of self-discovery and exploration, we have our own set of questions that relates to our unique journey. My backstory was that of an abused wife with young children, who had just escaped a violent and terrifying life—the help I was looking for was going to be different from a mother who had lost her son to drugs. Yes, we would both be looking for support, love, and understanding, but our fundamental questions would differ. My first question would be 'What do I do now to cope on my own?' The mother who is grieving for her son may be asking 'Why me? Why him? Why us?'

The answers we need are going to be dissimilar for obvious reasons. Eventually, both of us might be able to pick up the same book, something like Susan Jeffers' *Feel the Fear and Do It Anyway*, and it will speak volumes and motivate us both, but in the beginning, at the start of our self-help journey, we have very singular needs and this is why individual books will (and will not) work for you.

When I published my first book, *How I Changed My Life in a Year*, a lovely friend of mine took great pleasure in promoting it and recommending it to her family and friends. She loved what I'd done, how I'd done it, and how I told my story. Fast-forward to the sequel-that's-not-a-sequel, *How I Motivated Myself to Succeed*, and that same friend privately messaged me to say, quite honestly, that she didn't like it. Was I offended? No, of course not; every reader is entitled to their opinion. However, it helped me realise how essential self-help books are at specific points in our life. I know that my friend is fabulously organised, supports her local community, and is a busy mum to two young children. She bought and read my book to support me as a writer, for which I'll be eternally grateful, but the book itself was not what she needed in her life. It didn't speak to her in the same way my first book had.

So, this made me wonder if we are all as helpless as we think we are. I devoured self-help books because I felt lost, alone, and worthless. Somewhere along my life path, I'd allowed other people's opinions of me to define who I was and how I felt. My ex-husband's vicious tongue had left deep wounds, and I translated that into being a helpless woman.

As it happens, I've spent the last fifteen plus years as a single mother, running my own business, paying my bills, navigating the various dramas that come with growing children, and survived to tell the tale. I'm not a helpless woman; I'm a bloody warrior woman!

Have you ever felt helpless? Why did you? What or who made you feel this way? I found that keeping a journal helped me to piece together the trigger words and phrases that allowed me to fall into the victim role. It was interesting to see how I would, or could, fluctuate between victim, persecutor, and rescuer within any given situation.

Victims feel powerless and sway toward the "poor me" option. This is usually linked to a persecutor who blames them for any problems or tears them down and humiliates them. Can you see yourself in either of these roles? Perhaps you're more of a rescuer who rushes to everyone's side and tries to fix people? All these roles leave us helpless in one way or another. It's known as the "Drama Triangle" and is used by psychologists and counsellors across the world. If you want to delve deeper into this topic then I recommend you search for articles by Stephen B. Karpman, MD, who founded this psychological tool.

Understanding why you feel so helpless can be of great benefit when trying to improve your life or situation. Considering why someone close to you feels helpless is also worth investigation.

Let's try to understand what helplessness means. For most, it's an inability to change something meaningful in their life. It can also surface when you've lost all hope. If this is the case then I would strongly recommend that you see your GP. You may be suffering from depression, and having qualified support will help you manage your feelings and symptoms.

Other than depression, what else causes us to feel helpless?

Our past can cause us to feel this way. When we fail to deal with a situation or issue satisfactorily over and over, we pretty much teach ourselves how to be helpless. It might be that we don't have the skills to manage the problem, or we've absorbed those pesky limiting beliefs as truth. Any lack of control leaves us feeling uncomfortable. There is also the possibility that over time we've developed a unique talent for playing the helpless victim. I saw this time and again when I was training and when I ran my holistic spa. Some clients gained more attention from their vulnerability than by improving their health and well-being.

If sweet old Aunt Dotty is told by a respected surgeon that she has bad legs and needs to stay off them, she'll do as she's told. Family and friends will rally round to help, and over time the "patient" becomes dependent on this help. Aunt Dotty believes that she is helpless and that walking again is out of her control. If this person is usually isolated, or elderly, they may enjoy the attention they receive and worry that if they were healthy they would lose their friends and family and be alone again.

You might recognise this victim behaviour online too. Some of our social media contacts may feel disconnected. When they fill their newsfeed with doom and gloom about ill health, career choices, family drama, or relationship woes they are rewarded with likes and supportive comments from well-meaning followers. Why would they stop sharing if their victim mentality is giving them exactly what they crave and need? If that outlet were taken away from them, they would feel even more disconnected than they already do.

I've given many talks at personal development events about motivation, writing for healing, and my creative journey as a writer. Every now and then I'll come across one member of the audience who shares their troubles in graphic detail regardless of the fact there might be ten, twenty, or one hundred people listening to them. They feed off the exposure.

It can be far too easy to get sucked into this way of thinking and being. I've experienced this myself when I was going through various medical exams to discover what was wrong with me. Back in 2015, following an insect bite, my body started to misbehave. My limbs stopped working, I would fall asleep at all hours of the day, I was exhausted and in constant pain. Tremors were running through my legs. I felt like an alien had invaded my body, but nobody could tell me what was happening. I had numerous MRIs, a lumbar puncture, and more blood taken than a vampire could drink in a month. I wallowed in victim mode because I felt so awful. My depression and anxiety went through the roof, my symptoms flared, I developed insomnia, put on weight, and eventually hid away.

That is what I believe helplessness to be. I was terrified and lonely, and with every test coming back negative, I started to think I was going mad.

Eventually, I talked myself out of the victim mentality and began taking back control. Those feelings of helplessness began to fade as I took action. I planned my recovery, I took responsibility, and I began to turn my health around.

Reading, listening to music, and writing were important self-help tools for me at that time. The more I immersed myself in what I loved, the more in control I felt. There's an entire section about the self-help toolkit later on which is worth bookmarking.

What can you do to take back control if you are feeling helpless?

Here are a few things you could try:

- Switch off your phone/laptop for a full day. Disconnect from the online swarm of distractions and never-ending notifications.

- Create a vision board of your ideal life. Cut and stick images that represent what you want in your life/home/career to a board (see the section on creating a vision board if you're going to have a go).

- Get some exercise or fresh air. Walking by water or in the woods can be enough to lift your mood and help you feel more in control.

- Give yourself permission or the time and space to explore why you may be feeling helpless. Do you have a severe or essential, life-changing decision to make? When I finally decided to leave my abusive husband, it was a split-second decision. The words 'I want a divorce' came out of my mouth before I could overanalyse them.

- Gather your support network. Seek out those friends who you trust to be honest with you and tell them how you feel. You're not looking for them to fix your problems; instead, you need a supportive ear or a sounding board. When my depression was at its worst I discovered who my real friends were. I cut people out of my life, including all the negative online connections that sucked the energy out of me. Don't be afraid to declutter your social circle.

WHAT DOES YOUR BEST LIFE LOOK LIKE?

Every year I purchase too many planners and journals because I'm yet to find one that contains everything I love and need. Some of them have colouring pages, sales trackers, gratitude notes, and pretty covers, and others have goal stickers, inspirational quotes, and support pages on social media, but all of them are bright and colourful and help me to streamline my days. Being organised is something I require in my life as the structure keeps me sane.

Having primary appointments logged, as well as plenty of free space for spontaneity, takes away the stress of being a single mum, author, and businesswoman. I record my writing days as ruthlessly as my dental appointments, and always look forward to the entries that say 'coffee with friends.'

Stationery is an indulgence I can't deny. If I were to unwrap a carton of Post-it Notes on Christmas morning, I would be one very happy lady!

What does this have to do with living your best life, I hear you ask? I've explored many varieties of planners and I've always cherished the ones that offer space for personal development.

Yes, I need to record my appointments. Yes, I want to track my social media stats to check my marketing and book campaigns are working. Yes, I love the multicoloured ribbons that save the day. However, being able to do some self-work alongside the day-to-day running of my empire is always appreciated.

For me, living my most authentic life needs to contain a blend and a balance of the mundane and the extraordinary. By using paper products, I can see at a glance how my year (and my life) is playing out.

On my office wall, I have a year-at-a-glance wall calendar. The first thing I add is my manuscript submission dates so I know how much time I've got to work on my books. Next, I'll add holidays—a mix of work and play.

My best life, or my ultimate dream, would be to work from anywhere I want in the world. Barcelona beach would be perfect, as would a lakeside retreat in America, Italy, or the United Kingdom. I'd welcome the opportunity to chug through the Scottish Highlands in a VW camper van, exploring the incredible countryside and writing on the go. I certainly wouldn't turn down the chance of being paid to travel and write.

You may notice that I haven't mentioned my lovely children, family, friends, or my mischievous cat in these scenarios. That's because our best life is simply that—OURS.

Hidden amongst one of the shiny planners I bought years ago was an exercise that asked me to write a full page on what my perfect day would be from the moment I woke up right through until bedtime. At that time, I was hung up on doing what I *should* for the good of my family. That meant running around like a headless chicken getting my kids to various after-school clubs and playdates. I, Shelley Wilson, didn't exist. I was "so-and-so's mum."

The exercise asked me to think about myself and nobody else. To break from reality and dream about the kind of day that only happens in movies with shiny, happy heroines, soft music, and tantalising sunsets.

It took me a couple of attempts before I started to let go and let my imagination have fun. One variation saw me attending the Oscars with Johnny Depp, and in another, I was hired as an extra in a Marvel film. Once my creative juices were flowing I was able to craft my perfect day without the appearance of Captain America (although why you wouldn't want Chris Evans in your perfect-day scenario is a mystery to me), or Hollywood idols, and picture something that felt real.

My perfect day would start in a seaside cottage where my bedroom overlooked the water. I drank coffee on the porch in the early morning sunshine before walking to a local bakery for fresh bread and pastries. I'd write for hours and submit all my literary masterpieces to the many publications who wanted to work with me. I'd walk, paddle in the sea, read whenever I wanted, and enjoy lunch with friends. The day would finish with a sumptuous meal, a good book or a film night, and a walk along the beach.

Now, I adore my children and the fact that they didn't appear in my perfect day worried me at first. Mum guilt is real, and it can stop us from reaching for the sky, owning our dreams, and moving forward. It's an inbuilt instinct to put our children, or anyone else for that matter, ahead of our own needs, but I want you to consider that it's time to stop doing that. When I ran my holistic spa, I always told those clients who needed to justify doing something for themselves that they couldn't fix anyone else if they were broken. I've been broken, so I entirely relate to this statement. Think of your self-help in the same way as the flight attendant shares the safety instructions with you before takeoff. ALWAYS put on your own oxygen mask before helping others. This exercise can help you appreciate that.

I soon realised that the other point of doing this activity was to find out where your true passions lie, what interests you have, and what activities you crave. Being by water was vital for my self-care and well-being, and I understood that nature was how I filled my creative well, enabling me to be productive in my writing schedules.

I didn't mention my phone, shopping, driving in a busy commute, or tackling the big shop on a Saturday afternoon. Even now, if I close my eyes, I can see that cottage and hear the waves on the sand.

Now it's your turn. I want you to have a go at doing this exercise for yourself to see how powerful it can be in helping you discover your authentic self. If you're going to cast yourself in a Marvel film then go ahead. If you'd prefer to imagine yourself as a CEO of a law firm then do that. Maybe starting your own beauty business or retiring early would be more in line with your best life.

Start with a full day. Imagine you've just woken up at 7:00 a.m. (or 10:00 a.m. if having a lie-in is your ultimate dream) and then document everything you would love to do until you go to bed. Be as detailed as you can be. Who are you spending time with? Where are you? What are you doing?

I want you to visualise this perfect day. Close your eyes and see yourself doing whatever it is you've included. Daydream about the best way to fit everything in, bring your idea to life in your mind.

I've listed a few questions you can ask yourself to get started. Use the worksheet at the back of the book to write out your answers to these perfect day prompts. If you need more space, then grab a journal, a piece of paper, or a notebook and keep writing. I guarantee it will leave you feeling content and upbeat.

I briefly mentioned vision boards in the last section. Creating a visual representation of your ideal day can also be helpful as it's a constant reminder of all the things you cherish. I've included a section on making a vision board later if you want to try it out.

In the meantime, have a go at this exercise and feel free to let me know how you get on at *authorshelleywilson@gmail.com*.

My perfect day prompts:

Q. Where am I?

Q. Who am I with?

Q. What country am I in?

Q. What am I doing?

Q. What do I wish I could do every day?

Q. Who would I love to spend time with?

Q. If I could do any career/hobby in the world, what would it be?

Once you have an idea of what your perfect day looks like you can begin to implement elements of it into your real life. As I mentioned, water plays a big part in my self-care, so adding my holiday dates to my wall calendar allows me to see at a glance when I'll be going away next.

When I use the word "holiday," I don't necessarily mean expensive family package holidays, although I'm always eager to travel with my kids. More often than not I'll book weekend trips or overnight stays in various places across the United Kingdom. I live in the West Midlands, which is in the centre of England. It means I can get to any coast reasonably quickly within a few hours or explore the abundance of rivers and canals in my local area.

I'll happily travel solo, which means if none of my family or friends are free, I can still get away. Recently, I made a research trip to Northumberland for a young adult novel I was writing. I needed to see the landscape, smell the North Sea, and picture my fictional characters in my chosen setting. Not only did I get to embarrass my daughter by pretending to be an invading Viking and running up a sand dune, I also discovered a fabulous area of natural beauty. Spending a weekend in a gorgeous boutique hotel, where our bedroom overlooked the water, and visiting castles and historical sites brought parts of my perfect day to life, and in turn, it lifted my mood, provided necessary self-care, and allowed me to live my dream, albeit on a smaller scale.

What can you do today to bring your perfect day to life? Who can you call, or where can you go? If your budget is tight, you can look online for special last-minute deals on hotel rooms. Perhaps you have friends or family who live in another area, who would be happy to put you up for a few nights.

Do you have a happy place? Can you search for one in the local area that gives you that sense of escape or peace? I'm fortunate to live close to Kenilworth Castle in Warwickshire, England, which was visited by Queen Elizabeth I on her tour in 1575. It's an incredible place to visit, full of history and stories. I often refer to this as my happy place. When I can't get to the seaside I'll visit the castle ruins. Can you find something similar?

Build a picture in your mind of what your best life looks like, and then take action to make it happen. It doesn't matter how small the steps are that you choose, so long as you take them. One day I will live by the sea, a lake, or a river, but until then I'll continue to recreate my perfect day over and over.

BECOMING SELF-AWARE

Do you feel misunderstood? Do your family or friends look at you as if you've gone slightly crazy? Do you often feel like you're the odd one out?

There's a strong possibility that you are becoming self-aware, and everyone around you doesn't get it. They don't get *you*, or what you're trying to achieve.

Few of us like change. We feel safe in our ruts, even when they're not good for us. Stepping out of that comfort zone, no matter how uncomfortable life may be, can be more fearful than coping with a crappy existence.

When you begin to explore self-help or personal development, change becomes inevitable, and with that comes a slow evolution of self. You start to investigate your self-worth, your strengths, weaknesses, motivations, and beliefs. Life shifts and your emotions shift with it. What once excited you may now bore you. Someone you thought was important might no longer fill you with awe. This progression is perfectly normal.

Remember in the introduction when I told you that self-help had never been on my radar? At that point in my life,

I was as far from being self-aware as I could get. I had no clue who I was, what I wanted, or why I was the way I was. When I look back at the younger version of me, I cringe, not because of the bad eighties perm, although that was enough to make anyone weep, but because she was so distant. I had loads of friends, but I never really listened to them or helped them achieve and grow. I was told I was fun, which at the time would have been a compliment. Today, I see that as being disconnected and fake.

As a teenager and young adult, my mind operated on autopilot, which essentially meant that my habits, thoughts, and reactions controlled me instead of the other way around.

After my marriage ended, I was lost, lonely, scared, and suffering from ill health due to stress. My default setting allowed me to use distraction as a way of coping with the situation I found myself in. I drank myself into oblivion. Nowadays, we use social media to lose ourselves and often compare ourselves to the fake lives projected onto our newsfeed.

Over time I got better at recognising this. I still use books and movies to escape reality, but I've learned to come back to real life afterwards, and I now appreciate the need for a positive distraction. My struggle with food is ongoing, but I'm aware it's an issue, and I'm dealing with it.

Can you resonate with any of these actions? Have you used food, drink, drugs, or sex to dull the pain? Do you sit in front of your TV endlessly binge-watching your favourite shows?

To become self-aware means that we see the harm in certain distractions, and we choose what we want to do instead of operating on autopilot. Now, I love online streaming and can happily watch *Supernatural*, *Vikings*, or *The Tudors* for the gazillionth time when I need to switch off, but I also identify when I'm anxious or upset.

I read a fabulous article by author Mark Manson about distractions. He surmised that we are ignorant of how we use our time in the office, believing we are busy worker bees when in reality we function approximately three hours a day, and in our home life we are blissfully unaware of how disconnected we are. We think we listen, we think we show up and engage, but in truth we're pretty rubbish at all of it.

He also referred to the constant surfing on his phone, the absentminded way he flicked between platforms, forgetting that he had previously visited certain sites.

Can you relate? When I'm in this mindset (and we all do it), I'll check my open browsers on my phone as a way of reconnecting with reality. If there are ten pages open then I know I've probably just lost an hour or two of my life to cat memes and YouTube snippets.

If you're striving to become more self-aware, then you need to understand why and how you lost yourself in surfing the net or watching TV. Are you bored? Are you procrastinating? Are you avoiding something or someone? What are you fearful of?

Writing my books is something I love to do; preparing my blogs on the other hand (although they are considerably shorter—by about sixty thousand words in some cases) can occasionally send me into a spiral of distraction. I'll tidy up, clean the bathroom, sort out my shelves, declutter my desk, or rearrange my pens. I'll find *anything* to do other than write that blog post. Why? If I dig deep and discover why I act this way, then I can put strategies in place to help. Having a content planner and working to a monthly theme does the job.

Is there something you do on autopilot that you could explore? Do you make plans with friends and cancel at the last minute? Are you protecting yourself from something? Do you shy away from crowds or new experiences? Have you used food or drink to self-medicate? It's worth taking a bird's-eye view of your life to see if you're operating on autopilot.

I've given a few talks on motivation to women's business support networks and personal development groups and shared my thoughts on maintaining your motivational mojo. I believe that to stay motivated to complete any project or goal you need to know yourself (be self-aware).

To do that, I advise the audience to follow four simple steps: Appreciate your life story, write a journal, meditate, and ask for feedback. Let's explore each of these for a moment.

Appreciate your life story. I want you to remember this simple fact—you are amazing. From the day you were born, you've grown and developed physically, mentally, and emotionally. When you think back over your life what standout moments can you remember? Can you fully appreciate all the lessons, good and bad? Everything you've been through has made you who you are today. Appreciating your past and accepting your present helps you to become aware of who you are and how you can navigate your future.

I'm a big fan of genealogy, and so far I've traced my Wilson line to Mirfield, Yorkshire in 1805. All the branches of my tree are part of my life story too. What mannerisms have been passed down through the generations? What upheavals did my great-great-grandparents overcome to ensure my survival? Appreciate your life story, and if you feel drawn to recording your highs and lows then do so.

Write a journal. This is one of my favourite self-help tools. Noting down my thoughts and feelings helps me recognise those triggers that can derail my well-being, spark my depression, or set me up for a bout of negative distractions, such as overeating. It's worth remembering that your journal is private to you. This is where you record your thoughts. It's a safe space to share your fears and dreams, and to be honest with yourself.

Meditate. This is another go-to personal development tool that brings me great joy. I run meditation sessions for ladies in my local area, and I've also published a couple of books on the topic, the most recent being *Meditation for Children.* The benefits of meditation are hugely documented as it can bring about such a feeling of peace, balance, and calm to your life. If you hope to become more self-aware then tapping into that quiet space will genuinely help.

Ask for feedback. Getting to know yourself is vital if you want to become self-aware. However, we often miss some of our most important positive traits because we tend to focus on the negatives. When I look in the mirror, I see the bags under my eyes and the flecks of grey in my hair. When my sister-in-law looks at me she sees perfect eyebrows and wishes she could wear Converse and slogan T-shirts (yes, I'm nearly fifty, but I don't care!). Asking your friends, family, and colleagues for three words they associate with you can be a massive eye-opener.

On my private Facebook page, I remember asking my online friends what they thought I did for a living. I call myself an author, but I also run personal development workshops and work as a writing mentor. In all honesty, I was having a crisis of identity as I wasn't sure my marketing message was clear. I asked for feedback and was blown away by the results. Not only did the comments confirm that my friends also thought of me as an author, but they added words like inspiring, motivational, honest, and caring. My grin got wider and wider with every remark, and my self-awareness clicked in as I took on board the comments I received.

An interesting statistic that's worth sharing at this point is that we need to encounter three positive experiences to over-rule one negative. Think about that for a second. If I asked you to remember what happened to you last year, I bet you'll instantly recall an accident, bereavement, or some other negative moment. What about all the positives? If you experienced three positives to every negative then last year must have been pretty amazing!

Becoming self-aware helps us to help ourselves. We no longer feel helpless when we are in control of our lives. However, self-awareness also has a dark side.

A few years ago, I started attending counselling sessions. It only took me fifteen years to take the plunge and begin working with a qualified therapist to help me unravel my limiting beliefs and the trauma left behind by my marriage. I've done a lot of self-work over the years, most of it in association with my training in alternative therapies and healing. The counselling was (and still is) tough. I've cried so hard I never thought I'd stop. There have been some sessions when I've come home and crawled into bed mentally and physically exhausted. I keep going because I know deep down it's helping. My self-awareness has reached another level, and yet with that, I also realised that I was beginning to hate myself.

When we work on our self-awareness, it opens our eyes to the flaws (internal and external) that we have. I had a moment after one particularly bad day where I wished I'd never discovered self-help because I believed I'd been better off as a blinkered idiot oblivious to the world around me. I judged myself for being a well-rounded and evolved person, and I hated myself for it. It took me quite some time to realise that with self-awareness comes self-acceptance.

Would you say you were empathic? If you answered yes to this question, then you probably have healthy self-acceptance. By being able to accept your own mistakes you can see the flaws in other people and still treat them with consideration and kindness.

By accepting yourself, you embrace self-awareness and in turn, project love and genuine authenticity.

As I travel along this path of self-discovery, I must learn to accept myself for who I am and why I am the way I am, and to own my past mistakes—of which there are many. We all do what we can with the information we have at our disposal. When I started to train in holistic health and began to understand limiting beliefs I feared that I might have damaged my children beyond repair. However, as I uncovered self-awareness and talking to yourself in a positive way, I inadvertently taught my children how to be authentic, honest, and open. In turn, they will go on to show their own families how to rock a happy, authentic, balanced life.

Awareness is knowing what's going on around you, but self-awareness means understanding what you're experiencing and feeling.

I'm a huge advocate of meditation and find this to be the perfect starting point for becoming self-aware. We need to be grounded and centred to start the process; otherwise, we won't be able to learn and evolve. Tai chi and yoga are also great activities for becoming more mindful.

There are several exercises you can do to help with your self-awareness. Most of these are done in corporate environments to help employers synchronise their needs with potential employees, help support staff, and grow businesses. They're worth exploring for your personal needs. The first is the Myers-Briggs personality test. I've done this for myself as well as for my fictional characters in my young adult novels. The results are fascinating. The idea of the assessment is to help you understand what makes you tick and how you can use this knowledge in day-to-day life. You can easily find their test online.

Another assessment exercise you could try is the SWOT analysis. The idea here is to note down your strengths, weaknesses, opportunities, and threats. You might like to record your professional qualities and most significant achievements for strengths. For your weaknesses think about what you avoid doing, or something you'd like to learn how to do. When you consider opportunities think about education and learning new skills, who supports you, and how you can show yourself in the best light. Threats may include people or problems that get in the way of you succeeding or other obstacles you may face.

If the assessments seem a bit scary, then I'd suggest you start small and journal for four minutes a day. Jot down your thoughts, feelings, and emotions at the end of every day and keep checking back with yourself to see if you're making progress or coming up against the same problems over and over.

Becoming self-aware is a voyage of discovery and one you'll be glad you began.

REMOVE *SHOULD* FROM YOUR LIFE

Y ou've heard me refer to the word *should* quite a few times so
far in this book, and every time I've typed it out, it has made
me shudder. How can such a simple word be so disempowering?

What do you think about when you hear it? Does it take you
back to your childhood and teachers or parents telling you how
you *should* behave, or what you *should* do when you grow up?

Should strips you of all your power and comes from a sense
of obligation. There is no joy in life if you live by the word *should*.
Remember how we talked about our perfect day and what that
could entail? Did you feel enthusiastic as you dreamed up your
ideal home, career, partner, or lifestyle? That enthusiasm comes
from you living your most authentic life—it's a way of celebrat-
ing your higher self. When that enthusiasm wavers, or disap-
pears, it means you're operating at a lower frequency, and you're
at risk of adopting a humdrum existence without joy, peace,
and contentment.

Think back to your schooldays; were you told by career ad-
visors, teachers, or parental figures that you were not bright
enough or lacked confidence? Perhaps they branded you the

class clown or the chatterbox. Did they recommend that you *should* work in one industry instead of following your dreams in another? Maybe they told you to work in retail instead of opening a restaurant? Or perhaps they thought you *should* be a secretary instead of a supervisor. It's no wonder your enthusiasm vanished. Even reading about that makes my shoulders sag. I was at school in the eighties when it was still acceptable for an eraser to hurtle across a classroom if the teacher wanted to silence the class. Fortunately, things have changed dramatically, and teachers today are more aware of how actions and words can lift a student or demotivate them. It's always worth remembering that words have the power to heal and harm.

I want you to think about the conversations you've had recently. Has anyone said the word *should* to you? Have you said it to anyone else? I've had to stop myself on more than one occasion from saying it to my three children. I'm sure the parents amongst you can relate to that voice which pipes up when your offspring try and exert their independence.

'Oh my, are you sure you *should* wear that?'

'*Should* you catch the last bus home?'

'I think you *should* look at other university options. Timbuktu is so far away!'

We didn't have our children so we could turn them into puppets. We had them so they could grow, develop, and make a name for themselves in the world. Let them decide for themselves what they want to do—and then do the same for yourself.

How you talk to yourself is just as important. Do you hear yourself saying 'I *should* do that'? Try and notice when the *S* word creeps into your vocabulary.

Social media, although a wonderful tool for reaching friends across the globe, has its destructive side. A stylist friend of mine calls it *comparisonitis*, which I love. When we watch the newsfeed of acquaintances, family, friends, colleagues, and influencers sharing their best days, they are more often than not only showing us the good bits. Their entire life is edited, scripted, and fake. They believe that to be liked and accepted they *should* act a certain way. Of course, this leaves the rest of us thinking we *should* be doing something with our lives to compete.

I used to be guilty of this myself, sharing any achievements on my pages and lapping up the validation from external sources. Eventually, I started sharing the shitty days, and my struggle with depression, and instead of attracting white noise I was inundated with comments from grateful people who were glad it wasn't just them feeling low.

Don't fall into the trap of thinking you *should* keep up with the shiny, happy people who post stunning photographs of their summer holidays. Try posting one of your mosquito bites and see how different the engagement is then—you'll find a much more authentic conversation starts to flow.

I use the fabulous Happiness Jar self-help technique to remind myself of all the positivity and joy in my life, and steer away from all the "you *should* do this if you want to be happy." It's something anyone can do, and I would highly recommend you try it out.

Grab yourself an old jam jar and a small notebook. Decorate the pot if you want to make it extra special. Every time you do something that makes you happy write it on a scrap of paper and add it to the jar. I usually start this activity on January 1, but you can start it whenever you want. Over the year I'll add cinema ticket stubs, notes from my kids, and an abundance of handwritten notes with stuff I've done. I include things like coffee and cake with friends, laughing at something my children have done, visiting somewhere special, going to a concert, holidays, stroking the cat, visiting friends, good book reviews, etc. On New Year's Eve I tip out the jar and reread all the slips of paper. If you think you've had a lousy year this exercise will tell you otherwise. It's lovely to look back on all the positivity, fun, and happy moments that made up your year. You don't have to keep the notes as rereading them is the lift you need. Clear it out and start again the next day. Get your family to join in and see if the kids can add their happy moments to the jar too. It's a beautiful way to see how joyful your life is without needing to live how other people think you *should*.

HOW IMPORTANT IS MOTIVATION?

I get asked about motivation most days, and it still surprises me that my readers think I have it all figured out. I get stuff done, and I'm great at setting deadlines and goals and going after them, but I could still get an A in procrastination.

Motivation is necessary if we hope to develop ourselves as individuals. It's also helpful in our career or business as it's a driving force to success, but understanding how important motivation is in life can be useful when we are setting our goals, applying for jobs, or trying to establish a self-care routine.

Let me ask you a question. What does motivation mean to you? Use the worksheet at the back of the book to write out your answer or, if you prefer, write in your journal. Don't overthink it; write what comes into your head.

For me, it's the ability to get on with whatever project, job, or goal I have on at that moment in time. If I'm writing one of my books, then my motivation is to hit the submission deadline in good order. When I gave up alcohol over seven years ago my motivation was all about my mental and physical health. I wanted to feel better about myself, stop overanalysing my life (and hangovers in your forties and fifties are so much worse than when you were twenty). A runner uses race day to motivate themselves—you wouldn't run the London Marathon without training first. University students use the prospect of a well-paid career in the arena of their choice to knuckle down and study. Infants see their peers walking, talking, or using the toilet and it motivates them to do the same, with a little guidance and prompting from caregivers. We are all surrounded by reasons to stay motivated, and yet some of us find it incredibly challenging to do so.

In my book, *How I Motivated Myself to Succeed*, I shared a breakdown of what I believed motivation represented.

Here's a summary: it includes the necessity to remain **mindful** in everything you do, noticing what your body and mind are telling you, and being open to new opportunities that will inevitably come your way the more conscious and self-aware you are.

Looking at life through the eyes of a child, with innocence, allows us to remain **optimistic**. As adults, we can worry ourselves into a stress-induced frenzy, but what would happen if we switched off for just five minutes a day to nourish our inner child?

Trusting ourselves is another critical factor of motivation. If we harbour dark feelings about our capabilities then no amount of motivation, or inspiration, will help us. We must set aside those limiting beliefs and learn to trust in our abilities.

The power to change bad habits, to find happiness, and to love who we are is within all of us, and we need to tap into our **inner wisdom** to motivate ourselves to succeed.

In the previous section, we talked about **validation** and how the way we think we *should* live our lives can become a negative process. However, validation is also a valuable tool for motivating us to improve ourselves. We can look at other people who are further along their personal development journey than us and see the changes they've made, witness the positivity, and appreciate the work they've done to get to that place. They are providing us with the validation we need to prove that no matter what life throws at us, we will survive.

Taking **action** is probably the single most important part of motivating yourself. First, you need a desire to make a change, but that desire will never become a reality without the action steps in the middle. Think about it in terms of losing weight. You won't drop weight instantly overnight just by joining a slimming group; you need the steps in between and the dedication to see it through.

Thinking outside the box will help keep your motivation levels up. This might be changing the way you feel about something (exercising, for example) or taking a different approach. Come at your problems and fears from an alternative direction and see how your motivation levels shift.

Finally, by motivating ourselves, or finding a support network to keep us motivated, we achieve a sense of **empowerment**. Being around like-minded people, meeting new friends, and sharing that positive energy feeds us, fills our creative well, and helps us grow.

Understanding our motivation helps us to choose the right path. If you struggle to get out of bed in the morning and drag yourself to work, then you're not motivated in your career. It's like a flashing neon sign above the highway of your life saying STOP. NOTICE. CHANGE.

I still remember the drive to one of the places I worked when I was much younger. As my car approached the turning, I would start to feel hot and sick. The thought of spending the next eight or nine hours in that building filled me with dread. Have you ever felt like this? Do you feel like this now? It's torture and something that can drain you of all motivation, desire, and happiness. Is that how you want your life to be?

Motivation drives us to do better, to be better, and to want what's best for us in our career, life, relationships, and every other area of our existence. If you need more money so you can save and travel, then this is your motivation to ask for a pay rise or get a better-paid job.

What do you desire most in life? Use the worksheet at the back of the book to write out your answer or, if you prefer, write in your notebook. Are you desperate to write a book, start a family, take control of your finances, get married, travel, start a business, ask for a promotion, retire, adopt a dog, run a marathon, learn to speak French fluently, or something else?

Understanding what's important to you is vital. It allows you the space to explore the action steps you'll take to turn your dreams into reality. Motivation helps us to achieve those goals. It turns thought into action. Remember when we talked about our core values? Think about what you wrote down then and see if your desire matches up with your values. Motivation happens when your values link up with your sense of purpose.

Be the person that everyone wants to be around because you know how to self-motivate. Alternatively, find someone in your circle who motivates you, or makes you feel like you can do anything when you're with them. If you don't have anyone local, turn to podcasts, YouTube, books, and webinars and watch or listen to motivational people.

Yes, motivation is essential in everything we hope to achieve, but it also needs encouragement and nourishment. Think of it like an extra muscle in your body that needs to be worked daily so it grows strong and powerful.

Before I close this chapter, I wanted to quickly talk about motivation and depression. As someone who suffers from severe depression and anxiety, I've experienced firsthand the agony of feeling deflated, lost, and unmotivated to even climb out of bed, let alone achieve a goal. Author of *Self-Coaching: The Powerful Program to Beat Anxiety and Depression*, Joseph J. Luciani offers a fabulous way of dealing with depression and finding small ways to motivate yourself. He advises his readers to see depression as a habit rather than an illness. I found that idea quite compelling as it put me back in control of my mind and life. I've stopped saying that I have depression (apart from in this book as it's relevant to the topic) because my constant "I am depressed" talk was fuelling the fire. When I picked up *The Secret* all those years ago, the first lesson I learned was that thoughts become things. If I talk negatively then I'll attract more negativity. If I change it up and start talking more positively I'll attract good things. It works, I promise.

Becoming more self-aware also helps to combat depression as you begin to live in the now rather than mulling over what is upsetting you, or why you are feeling low. My internal chatty parrot never shuts up, ever! I need to manage my self-care and continue my personal development journey so I can be more mindful. This, in turn, helps me to control my mood and deflect the black fog that used to descend on me so quickly.

One of the biggest wins for me was learning to accept tiny successful moments. Not forgetting to buy toothpaste, making a single book sale, or getting the washing in before it rained were all excellent ways of recognising the good in life and pushing the depression to the sidelines. With every little win my motivation for life began to emerge.

If you struggle with depression but want to find your motivational mojo, I'd suggest you jot down all the things you could do to help yourself reconnect with the world. Ask a friend to go for a coffee, go off-line for a day, take a walk outside, or delegate/ask for help.

Take time out when you need it but try using these tips and techniques to help navigate yourself back toward the light.

HOW TO HANDLE A BAD DAY

This section is a short one because none of us wants to dwell on our bad days. However, we all recognise that they exist and that's why I wanted to include them in this book. When we are starting on our self-help journey, especially if we've hit rock bottom before that journey begins, we can feel like one bad day follows another.

The most important lesson I want you to take away from this section is that it's okay to have a bad day. It's okay to feel shitty, sulk for a few hours, cry, rant, and scream. It's perfectly normal to wallow in self-pity, eat a massive tub of ice cream, snap at the family, or throw your phone across the room (although this action might be a tad expensive and inconvenient to keep doing). Where problems arise is when we stifle our feelings, when we shove our emotions deep inside and refuse to show the world that we're upset, angry, or sad.

We all have bad days, and it's okay. Repeat that sentence out loud. We ALL have bad days, and it's OKAY.

How you handle that day can be very different depending on the circumstances. If you're zipping through the streets in the back of an ambulance, then your bad day will be slightly different from someone who just got a parking ticket.

Let's assume you are safe and sound, and your bad day is down to waking up late, laddering your tights, or losing your keys. Shit happens. The world continues to turn. Stop for a second and take a deep breath in for the count of five and then release it through your mouth. Do this a few times until you're feeling stable. So, you've overslept—call ahead and apologise in advance for being late. So, you've laddered your tights—change them, go bare-legged, or wear trousers. When we take a moment to stop and breathe, we can begin to look at our bad day from a much calmer angle and find rational answers.

What if your bad day is slightly more serious? This is when self-help techniques can be beneficial. It's during a bad day when everything you've learned comes to the forefront and begins to make sense. Now you can appreciate how valuable it is to reach out and ask for help. Give yourself clear instructions about what you want to do, need to do, and are comfortable doing if and when you experience a bad day. I'm fortunate that I have a supportive friend who I can call in any situation and know she's got my back, whether that's talking me down from a rant, picking me up from the roadside, or buying the coffee and supplying the Kleenex. I'm there for her, and she's there for me—it's like an unwritten pact between us.

Do you have someone you can call on? Talking about the tough times, be it a bad day or a stressful situation, is how we begin to take control of our lives. None of us wants to feel helpless, alone, or lost, so we need to establish rules for ourselves that allow us to cope.

Next time you're having a bad day try doing something different. Deal with it in a new way and remember the breathing exercises.

If you suffer from depression then your bad days may feel like the walls are closing in on you. If this is you right now repeat the sentence from above. It's okay to have a bad day. If you need to stay in bed then stay in bed but reach out and tell just one person that today isn't a good day for you so they can gently bring you back into the world when you're feeling up to it.

WHAT'S PERSONAL ABOUT DEVELOPMENT?

Y ou will have noticed by now that self-help, personal growth, and development is a unique journey. Only you know what you want in life, what your desires are, who you want to spend your time with, and what you want to achieve. Nobody can make these decisions for you, and if they do, then you need to take your power back.

If you bought this book because you've had moments of helplessness and need a guiding hand back toward the light, then I hope this chapter provides you with the tools to make that happen. Whether you feel helpless or not, we all benefit from a physical "check-in" with ourselves now and then. What I mean by that is getting out of your head (shutting up the poisonous parrot for half an hour), and digging deep into who you are, what you want, and why you want it.

I've included a series of questions for you below that will hopefully help you find that personal link to your development. Don't jump on the well-being wagon if you're not 100 percent committed to the journey. If you're exploring self-help because someone said you *should* then consider what we've already covered. I love the quote 'when the student is ready, the teacher appears,' as it resonates so much with what self-help is all about. When you need it, or when you're ready to understand, the right tools will come your way. It's the Law of Attraction in full flow.

Dig deep and find that link to why self-help is personal to you. Only then will you reap the benefits and become more self-aware.

Have a go at answering the questions below. Use the worksheets at the back of the book or write in your journal. There are no right or wrong answers, only your authentic response. Don't think too hard before answering; just go with your gut instinct and write the first thing that springs to mind. This exercise is for you and you alone, and it's a way of exploring who you are, what you want out of life, and where you would like to be in the future. Be open and honest with yourself.

Q. What would you do if you were brave enough?

Q. What have you done that you never thought you would/could?

Q. Describe a spontaneous action that led to something incredible.

Q. What challenges are you ready to face?

Think back to the earlier chapter about describing your perfect day (What does your best life look like?). We were creative with our time for that exercise, but what if you only had an hour, afternoon, or weekend to spare? Jot down what you'd love to do with a short amount of time.

Q. What would you do if you had a spare hour?

Q. What would you do if you had a spare afternoon?

Q. What would you do if you had a spare weekend?

We talked earlier about experiencing three positive events to rule out one negative. Now I want you to tap into that positivity and recall your achievements. Remember, they don't have to be life-changing events. If you made it to work without laddering your tights then that can go on the list!

Q. What achievements (big or small) are you most proud of?

Most of us may associate achievement and success with our skills or career. There is nothing wrong with that but remember that your abilities and talents extend to every area of your life. Something you have a natural aptitude for may open up opportunities in life that you'd never considered before. Use the next few questions to think about those skills.

Q. What would you like to learn if time and money was no issue?

Q. What are you good at?

Q. What would you like to improve?

You can't have a self-help book without mentioning the *S* word—stress. We all suffer from varying degrees of stress, and we all cope with it in our own unique way. I remember when I ran my holistic health spa I had a regular reflexology client who would talk about her job throughout the session. She was in a high-powered, well-paid, exceedingly demanding role and yet she thrived on the stress of it all. I was exhausted just listening to her typical day in the office, but she loved it, and it shone through in her voice, expressions, and mannerisms. We all deal with things differently, which is why our friends and family can be a great help when we're struggling with something. What tips one person over the edge might be a slight bump in the road to someone else. Understanding yourself and how you cope with stress allows you to help yourself. You can feel more prepared and in control when you know your limits.

Q. What causes you stress (job, finances, relation ships, health)?

Q. What does that stress feel like for you (mentally, physically, and emotionally)?

Q. How do you currently cope with stress?

Q. What strategies would you like to implement in your life to combat/deal with stress?

It might be odd to think about the online platforms that bring us a stream of cat memes and random fake news stories as a stressor. However, your online activity can have a significant impact on your mental health, and don't even get me started about the impact social media has on our youngsters!

It's easy to get sucked into a time slip of two, three, or four hours staring at a screen, liking funny quotes, retweeting stories, pinning random stuff, or Boomeranging your dog for Instagram. Have you ever thought long and hard about the time you spend online, the platforms you're using and the content you're reading, and how that impacts your life? The next set of questions may bring up some scary statistics for you—be honest.

Q. How long do you spend online every day?

Q. How often do you use social media?

Q. If you set aside time for a social media break, what would you miss?

Q. What could you do instead if you weren't online?

Understanding motivation is a topic that fascinates me. Over time I've learned to appreciate when I feel motivated intrinsically (this is when we are driven by an internal desire, passion, or enjoyment for something), and when I'm extrinsically motivated (this is when we are driven by an external validation or reward). I was quick to discover that writing, for me, is a mix of intrinsic and extrinsic motivation. I love writing for the enjoyment of it, but I'm also a businesswoman and need to sell books to pay my bills.

The next set of questions will ask about who or what motivates you. Take time to think about your answers. Are you motivated by your colleagues, friends, and family, or is there a celebrity or guru who inspires you to do better? Has someone come into your life for a short time but left a huge impact? All these answers become the jigsaw puzzle of our life.

Q. Who motivates you?

Q. What keeps you motivated?

Q. Who do you admire?

Q. Who do you miss?

Q. What's the best piece of advice you've ever been given?

Let's take a moment to tap into our inner child, which is that unconscious part of us that is neither physical nor literal, but hugely powerful nonetheless. Everything that happened to us or around us when we were children will have had an impact on our adult life, whether we are conscious of it or not. Freud identified that this part of us could be responsible for our destructive behaviours and our mental health issues. Problems arise when we don't allow our inner child to come out and play, or we let them take over our adult personality. If we can learn to relate to our inner child, just like a parent would do with their actual child with discipline, structure, boundaries, and fun, then we can support ourselves and our self-help journey. We all get older, but do we ever grow up? It's a good reminder to add some fun and laughter into our lives.

Here's a frightening statistic for you. Children laugh approximately four hundred times a day. Adults laugh almost four times a day. Let that sink in for a minute. Wow! Now, imagine how much more enjoyable life would be if we allowed our inner child to emerge more acceptably, without the destructive possibilities or the adult temper tantrums.

The next set of questions allows you to tap into that part of you that may be suppressed. Also, don't shy away from treating your mini-me to a go on the swings, or letting them splash through the puddles; they'll thank you for it.

Q. What do you treasure most in the world?

Q. What did you learn in childhood that has sustained you through life?

Q. How do you treat others?

Q. How do others treat you?

Q. How do you treat yourself?

Q. What is your proudest moment?

Q. What is your funniest memory?

Q. What is your most embarrassing moment/memory?

Let's finish up with a "dream big" exercise. The next set of questions allows you to explore what interests you have, the places you would love to visit, and what passions you have in your heart. Dream big, write whatever comes to mind, no matter how out there it might seem, and step into your authentic self.

Q. What countries would you like to visit?

Q. What is your ideal job?

Q. What activities/hobbies would you like to try?

Q. If money was no issue, what would you like to do most with your life?

I hope you've enjoyed answering these questions. Remember, there are no right or wrong responses, only you being authentic, honest, and owning your personal development journey. It can be useful to redo them from time to time to assess how you're feeling, and to check if your goals and desires have altered. As we become more self-aware and advance on our path, our lives ebb and flow, and changes are inevitable. Don't avoid these changes; instead, use the questions above to reassess where you are.

MY 31-DAY SELF-HELP TOOLKIT

We've established that self-help begins with us, and how we help ourselves is going to be a personal choice. I mentioned earlier that it's not all about bubble baths and duvet days, but if that's what you need to help you find that inner calm and balance then go for it! Fill your bath, change your sheets, and fully embrace that self-help quest.

If you want to explore alternative ways to help yourself, then this 31-day toolkit will give you something different to think about every day of the month. If there are any suggestions that don't resonate with you then mix it up to suit your needs. I'm not a gym bunny (my first week was a bit of a disaster when I did try it—enrolled on Monday, received an introduction class on Tuesday, and was taken away in an ambulance on Friday!). However, going for a long walk around my neighbourhood is something I can do without the need for paramedics with gas and air. But before I show you what's in my toolkit, I want to tell you why it's so important to have one in the first place.

Why use a toolkit? I'm glad you asked. Throughout my holistic training and the subsequent years I spent running my spa, maintaining my CPD, and doing lots of self-work, I was able to include elements of this toolkit without even thinking about it. I refer to it as my "box of tricks." Writing in my journal, meditating, switching off, and winding down were as normal to me as brushing my teeth. When I fell ill, and my depression and anxiety exploded, my toolkit sat forgotten in the deep, dark recesses of my mind. I went so far the other way (sulking and wallowing in victim mode) that I forgot what it was like to look after my mental and physical health. It was my counsellor who reminded me of the importance of including self-care and self-love into my life once more.

If you've picked up this book because you didn't know where to start on the self-help road map, or you're just beginning to understand that self-help is an integral part of your personal development, then the prospect of doing something new every day for 31 days might feel awkward, uncomfortable, or overwhelming to you.

Don't think about this as a chore, or something else to fit into your already packed schedule. Do what you can, when you can, and don't put any additional pressure on your shoulders. Self-help for the helpless is all about taking it slow, understanding *why* you might need to help yourself, and finding the right route to match your lifestyle.

If you can tick one item off the list each week for a month then that's fabulous—well done. If you only do a self-help task at the weekends then that's brilliant—what an incredible weekend you'll have. If you fully embrace this toolkit and complete all 31 suggestions then you're going to have so much to work with in the future. These days, I consciously add at least three self-help toolkit tasks to my diary, and I'll wing the rest on an ad hoc basis. If I'm busy then I might struggle to go for a walk, cook a fancy meal, or escape to the seaside, but I know that I can spend four minutes before bed writing in my journal, or I can do a ten-minute meditation in the morning.

You'll be amazed at how easily these tasks become a habit when you make an effort to fill your life with time-outs and nourishing moments.

Below you'll find the 31-day list. I've also included a bit of space at the end for you to add your own items. There might be something you do or want to do that fills your creative well, brings joy to your life, and makes you feel content. If that's the case then incorporate this into your life—it's your life and your journey after all.

Read the list and see if anything resonates with you. Can you fit something in today, or tomorrow if you're reading this at night? Do you already do one of these tasks and never associated it with self-help? Most of all, enjoy the process. Self-help should be a natural occurrence and something you look forward to doing.

1. Cook a special recipe and take time to enjoy it (alone, or with friends/family)

2. Take a night off and order your favourite takeaway

3. Call a friend and arrange to meet them for a leisurely coffee and cake

4. Spend an hour at the gym, an exercise class, or go for a swim

5. Sit outside at night and watch the stars

6. Watch a sunrise or sunset—try to enjoy the moment rather than capturing it on your phone for social media

7. Go off-line for an hour, a day, or a weekend—no cheating

8. Spend four minutes during the day, or at night, to write in your journal

9. Visit the beach

10. Allow yourself an hour to read a magazine or a book

11. Get an early night or have a lazy morning and sleep late

12. Declutter one cupboard, bookshelf, or room in your house

13. Do something arts and crafts-related—knitting, colouring in, sewing, making soaps, jewellery, or mosaics

14. Turn on the radio or play your favourite albums or playlists LOUDLY and dance around the house until you're out of breath and smiling

15. Go for a drive without any destination in mind

16. Enjoy a twenty-minute nap

17. Spend an hour planning out your perfect holiday—even if you don't book it, you can plan it out, price it up, and dream about the day you make it happen

18. Spend time in your garden getting your hands dirty. If you don't have a garden get yourself a couple of house plants and make a window box

19. Say no to someone or something that doesn't bring you joy

20. Spend time researching a topic that fascinates you—you might be surprised at what you discover or what it leads to

21. Have a spa treatment such as a massage, facial, manicure, or pedicure

22. Write a letter to your sixteen-year-old self

23. Get dressed up in your favourite outfit, do your hair and makeup, and go out for a spontaneous lunch date either on your own or with friends

24. Write yourself a to-do list of all the irritating tasks you keep putting off and then spend one hour ticking off as many as possible

25. Go to yoga, Pilates, or Zumba class

26. Binge-watch your favourite TV series

27. Indulge in a Boxing Day at any time of the year. This is something Peter Jones, author of *How to Do Everything and Be Happy*, regularly does. He blocks out a full day in his calendar and only decides on the morning of that day what he plans to do. Be spontaneous with your Boxing Day. If you want to stay in bed watching old movies, do that; if you want to jump in your car and visit a castle, do that. The rules are don't plan and do whatever feels right

28. Get up an hour earlier than the rest of the household and enjoy a peaceful morning coffee or breakfast alone

29. Meditate—there are a variety of wonderful apps you can use to meditate on the go. I highly recommend Headspace and Calm

30. Go to your local park and play on the swings—nourish your inner child

31. Buy yourself a beautiful bouquet of flowers

Now add your own ideas to the list:

1.

2.

3.

4.

5.

What do you think? Have you found something that excites you? Don't be afraid to step outside of your comfort zone and pick one or two that you wouldn't usually choose. I remember sitting in my garden one autumn night and staring up at the stars as they blinked into life above me. My daughter wandered out to see what I was doing and when I told her I was stargazing she took a seat next to me and mimicked my actions. We sat there, wrapped up against the chill, for about an hour, watching the sky darken and the stars emerge. We chatted about space, the enormity of the universe, Peter Pan (second star to the right!), and the existence of alien life. It was a simple moment, an hour out of my day, but I remember it with such fondness and warmth that I often venture outside to stargaze when I need to switch off from a busy day.

Be open to what each task can lead to. There are opportunities around us to expand and explore our knowledge, skill set, and development. Maybe going to one yoga class ends up being the turning point you needed, and you train to be an instructor and start your own community group. Perhaps you start meditating and the anxiety you've struggled with for months begins to lift. I love researching topics of interest as I'm a typical Gemini and get excited about learning new things. I'm obsessed with Viking history to the extent that I wrote my young adult novel *The Last Princess* using my research notes. Don't think about the self-help toolkit as tasks you *must* do to help yourself, think of them as nuggets of wisdom, learning tools, and fun activities.

Self-help doesn't have to rock your world, and it doesn't have to be a massive shift in your mental health or a turn-around of your entire lifestyle. It can be small moments of pleasure: a giggle with your kids, stroking a pet, escaping to the movies, a walk in the park. Fill your box of tricks with what matters to you, and more importantly, fill your days with these activities until they become the norm.

CREATING A VISION BOARD

I've referred to vision boards a few times in this book because I see firsthand through my workshops the benefits of creating a vision board to manifest your desires.

If your personal development is important to you, then I hope you'll enjoy this short activity as it will provide you with a visual reminder of what you want to be, do, and have in your life.

In basic terms, a vision board is a collage of images and words. If you'd rather not get involved with cutting and sticking then you may prefer to use Pinterest and create an online vision board. Collecting empowering phrases, inspirational quotes, and powerful imagery can be done just as well on a digital platform as in real life—it's not quite as much fun though!

In short, a vision board is a powerful manifestation tool. The purpose of using a board is to activate the Law of Attraction and manifest the life you desire. I discovered the power of vision boards after reading *The Secret* all those years ago, and it's a tool I've used every year since.

If you fancy having a go at making your own board, then here's a list of items you'll need (don't worry, this exercise can be done on a budget):

- Noticeboard or large piece of cardboard

- Assortment of magazines

- Glue

- Scissors

Once you've gathered your supplies, I want you to start flicking through the magazines you've collected. While doing so, think about your answers to the questions from the earlier section (What's personal about development?). What do you want in life? Where do you want to be? Who do you want to spend your time with? Remember, your vision board is unique to you.

At this stage, all you are looking for are images, quotes, or words that resonate with you and make you smile. You may see a photograph in a magazine of a pregnant woman, and this might represent your desire to start a family. An image of feet wearing fluffy slippers might be the ideal reminder to relax on a Friday night and unwind. You'll interpret each image in your own unique way, and that's great.

Cut out and collect all the images you feel a pull toward. Sometimes it might not be clear why you've chosen a particular picture but follow your gut instinct.

Once you've got them all together, lay them out on top of your noticeboard or cardboard but don't stick them down just yet.

Do the images still resonate with you? Are some of them not quite as powerful as before? This is normal; set them aside and move to the ones that evoke an emotion.

When you've played around with the layout, and you're happy, then you can start to stick the images down. Keep going until every inch of space is covered.

Congratulations, you've just created a vision board.

When you're finished, place it somewhere you'll be able to see it every single day. To activate your vision board, you need to be looking at it often, visualising the images coming true, and taking action to make them happen. If you've always wanted to go on a cruise and your board has pictures of ships and the sea all over it, this will act as a daily reminder of your ultimate desire. Seeing these colourful pictures may spur you on to ask for extra shifts at work, or a pay rise; they might push you to sell all the junk you've got in your loft or basement. All that extra money can go in your cruise fund. This is how you manifest your dreams.

Don't be afraid to share it with your family and friends. Be proud of the life you want to manifest.

ALTERNATIVE THERAPIES

By now you will have a better understanding about self-help and how you can use a variety of tools and shift your mindset to take control of your life. It takes a strong person to admit that they need help and to act for the good of their mental, physical, and emotional health, and you've done that. You are that strong person.

There is an abundance of ways we can help ourselves, and I've touched on only a small number of tools that you can add to your personal development toolkit. What I want to share in this section are the fabulous alternative therapies that can support your journey, boost your energy and feel-good, happy hormones, and give you that all-important time-out.

For seven years, I ran a successful ladies-only holistic spa. At the time of closing my business I had an eight-month waiting list and a well-established client list. So many ladies appreciated the benefits of looking after themselves, and I found that working in this field was a joy. I felt honoured to be a part of my clients' self-care. My reasons for closing that business were health-related, and it was something my clients watched unfold, so when I made the difficult decision to cease trading they were supportive and understanding of my situation. What did interest me was how so few of my ladies found another therapist to take over their self-care. Yes, a part of me was filled with pride that they loved my little spa, the treatments I offered, and me as a therapist, but it also helped me realise how much our habits can keep us focused.

We talked about habits earlier, and the need to include some (or all) of the 31-day toolkit into your life. When my clients came for a treatment, I always made sure they booked in for the next week or month before they left. Their appointments became habit. They were embracing their self-care and looking after their well-being for the long term.

In this section, I want to highlight some of the fabulous self-care alternative therapies that are available to you. This is by no means an exhaustive list. I'm qualified in most of these therapies (excluding acupuncture and aromatherapy) and have experienced them from a position of giving and receiving. It has always been important to me to only recommend those therapies, books, podcasts, and tools that I have tried and tested myself. Only then can I know I am passing on the best advice to help you survive and thrive.

Have a read-through of the information below, tick off the therapies that you've tried, and search for a local spa or independent therapist who can deliver those you'd like to try next.

With most treatments, it's wise to complete a course of approximately six weeks so you can track any changes, improvements in health, or issues. Your therapist will advise you on this and support you throughout. Make sure you find a fully qualified and insured individual. There are far too many courses running, both online and in real life, where you can qualify in a weekend. I would advise only visiting a therapist who has completed the recommended number of case studies, holds a recognised qualification, and who is signed up with an association such as the FHT (Federation of Holistic Therapists).

Recommendations and word of mouth are a valuable way of finding a therapist to work with. Bonding with this person is vital as you are working together for the good of your health. If something doesn't feel right, leave. If you have an instant connection, then you'll begin a beautiful relationship.

I decided to train in beauty treatments as well as alternative therapies as this gave me the ideal platform to convert ladies who were unsure if holistic treatments were for them. Very often I would turn a pedicure client into a reflexology client, a facial client into an Indian head massage treatment client, and be able to gently persuade a body massage client into trying a Reiki session. My entire ethos was to help raise awareness of alternative therapies by allowing my ladies to dip their toes into the world of self-care, try it for themselves in a safe and reassuring environment, and make the decision for themselves.

Try what you feel comfortable with, but don't shy away from having a go at something different. You'll be amazed at what you might discover.

Acupuncture—Acupuncture is an ancient Chinese therapy often referred to as TCM (traditional Chinese medicine). There are many fully qualified independent therapists across the globe who work within a strict code of conduct and offer acupuncture for pain relief. The treatment itself involves thin needles being inserted into the body, limbs, and face where necessary. The needles are so fine that the client rarely feels them as they are inserted. The benefits of such a treatment are well-documented and include relief for pain and inflammation. It may sound quite frightening to imagine yourself lying on a couch covered in needles, but it's one of the most powerful therapies I've ever experienced.

Aromatherapy—Aromatherapy uses plant essential oils for therapeutic purposes. A therapist will be fully qualified in the right use of these oils and their carriers and understand the specific properties of each essential oil and how it can be applied. It's believed that the essential oils are absorbed directly into the body through the skin and lungs, allowing us to benefit on a mental, physical, emotional, and spiritual level. Although you can use essential oils in your bathwater (no bubbles though), room diffusers, or as a compress, most people will prefer to book an aromatherapy massage where your therapist will apply the oils to your skin as part of a relaxing and rejuvenating massage treatment.

Crystal Therapy—I have been fascinated with crystals from a young age and even gifted my mum a selection of blue crystals when I was eight years old to make her feel better when she had a sore throat. It was thirty years later that I realised blue crystals are the perfect stone to use for the throat chakra (and sore throats). A chakra is an energy centre in the body; it's believed that individual crystals can stimulate each chakra. Crystals are said to have their own vibrational energy, which helps to rebalance any disturbances or issues in the body's energy levels. Treatment can be as varied as the therapist giving it. Some will place crystals on you (you are fully clothed), and others will put them in a grid formation around you.

Hopi Ear Candling—A simple yet effective therapy that can be beneficial for migraine sufferers, swimmers, and frequent flyers. Push aside any thoughts of church candles and hot wax. An ear candle is a hollow tube usually made of cotton hardened with beeswax and essential oils. You lie on your side, and the therapist positions the candle in the opening of the ear (not inside the ear canal) before lighting the opposite end. It's a pleasant treatment as you can hear the crackle and pop of the flame as it slowly and gently burns the candle. Your therapist stays with you throughout to ensure the open flame is safe and controlled. The treatment is carried out on both ears and takes about half an hour.

Emotional Freedom Technique—Emotional Freedom Technique (EFT) can also be referred to as tapping and is like acupuncture in the way that it works with the energy flow of the body via meridians (an invisible flow of energy that runs from head to toe), although with EFT there is no need for needles; instead, the therapist will tap (using their fingertips) on specific points of the hands, body, head, and face to help rebalance any disruptions to the flow. It's believed that any illness or injury in the body or any psychological disturbance can interrupt the energy. By tapping on certain points, a therapist can bring about balance, enabling the energy to return to normal and essentially allowing the issue to disappear. I've trained to level two in EFT and can't begin to recommend this therapy enough. It's one of those treatments that must be seen or experienced to be believed. I ran a tapping workshop for a junior school year group many years ago as they got ready to sit their SATs and the children took to it incredibly well. We were able to work on the fears and worries they had about exams and moving to high school, leaving them feeling more in control.

Foot Reading—I was fortunate enough to attend a training course in foot reading by the founder of this therapy, Jane Sheehan, and was quick to sign up after watching Jane giving a demonstration at a Mind, Body, Spirit fair one year. In basic terms, foot reading is the art of analysing a person's feet and using the structure and texture, blemishes, moles, and nail health (and varnish colour!) to identify a client's personality and emotions. Jane has written many books about the subject, and I can highly recommend her first book, *Let's Read Our Feet!*

Reflexology—Reflexology is my favourite alternative therapy to give and receive. This gentle and relaxing treatment leaves you feeling like a new person. In reflexology, it is believed that the soles of the feet, as well as the top and sides, can be used as a map of the body. By working over specific areas (reflex points) of the feet, the therapist aims to rebalance the body. In a treatment, the therapist will be seated by your feet; they will also cleanse and massage your feet and lower legs as part of the procedure.

Reiki—Another alternative therapy that needs to be experienced to be appreciated is Reiki. I trained to Master Teacher level, which means I am qualified to teach Reiki, an honour that any teacher must never take lightly. It's worth noting that anyone can learn Reiki; you don't have to practise it as a career option. Reiki is passed on from master to student, and all students go through an attunement process to accept the Reiki energy. When I trained at level one it was for self-work and my own personal development. What it opened up for me was mind-blowing, which is what led me to invest in my studies and continue through the four levels.

The literal meaning of Reiki is 'universal life energy,' and it is believed that a therapist can draw on this healing energy, channelling it for the client to bring about balance and peace. As with most alternative therapies, Reiki works with the body's energy centres (chakras) to balance the flow. It's a profoundly calming treatment that lasts about an hour but leaves you energised for much longer.

There are so many other approaches you could try, from the Bowen technique, hypnotherapy, craniosacral therapy (CST), Neuro-Linguistic Programming (NLP), kinesiology, to deep tissue massage. The choices are endless, and they're yours to make. Building a regular self-care routine into your life will benefit you on a mental, physical, and emotional level, allowing you to survive and thrive.

You deserve the best in life and a life that is full of energy, laughter, hope, and authenticity. Only you can make the necessary changes to allow that to happen, so open yourself up to trying a few alternative therapies and see how they, and your chosen therapist, can support you on your self-help journey.

A FINAL WORD ON EMBRACING CHANGE

It's my hope and desire that if you picked this book because you felt helpless, that you now feel more in control, a lot brighter, and ready to embrace a positive future.

When something changes you, or you suffer from illness, grief, or abuse, it's perfectly normal to entertain feelings of despair, sadness, and pain. You enter a period of helplessness that can sometimes feel endless. But the darkness that hovers in your peripheral vision doesn't have to descend, and the self-sabotage doesn't have to rule your life; the low self-esteem and destructive language you use on yourself can turn into words of love and kindness.

Giving up or hiding yourself away can feel like the right option, but you've read this book, you've had a go at the exercises, and you were brave enough and strong enough to walk into a bookshop, or search an online book platform to find something that could help—you've started on a path of healing.

Everything I write comes from the heart. It also comes from experience. We can make a pact, together, to stop feeling helpless and to help ourselves to survive and thrive. I'm on this journey with you, whether that's in spirit or via my social media platforms and blog. Together we can learn to smile and laugh again, we can try out the toolkit or add our own variations, we can surround ourselves with positivity and good vibes, and most of all, we can step into our personal power and become the strong people we deserve to be.

Embracing the changes we want to make, as well as the changes that will inevitably happen as we become more self-aware and self-loving, is what self-help is all about. Help yourself to survive, help yourself to thrive, and help yourself to leave behind any feelings of helplessness.

You are amazing, and I believe in you!

SEEKING EXTERNAL HELP

Looking after our mental and physical health is more important than ever before. We are living longer and deserve to be fit and healthy into our twilight years. You've taken the first step on your self-help journey, and this will build over time to create the authentic life you love and deserve.

I've talked about depression and anxiety in this book and I wanted to mention that there are many support groups available around the world. You don't need to feel alone. Luckily with the internet, doing a search online will help you find the services that you are seeking and I would encourage you to reach out to these organisations if you feel you need them.

The books I write are to inspire, motivate, and teach as well as entertain my readers, and I enjoy including real-life anecdotes, and lessons I've learned on my own personal development quest, especially humour. As such, I chose to call this book *Self-Help for the Helpless* as a way of lightheartedly approaching the topic. However, I am fully aware of how destructive those feelings of helplessness can be. I've lived through it myself and can sympathise, but I've worked hard to pull myself back from the brink, and as part of my recovery, I found my smile and sense of humour, which has really helped get me through this. It was something I thought I'd lost forever, as I became more disconnected from the world around me, and the people in it. Helplessness is serious and if you feel this way then I urge you to reach out, if not to available support groups, then to a trusted friend or family member.

Support of any kind is paramount to maintaining our mental, physical, emotional, and spiritual well-being, and it's a process that needs to be nurtured.

WORKSHEETS

MY PERFECT DAY PROMPTS

Q. Where am I?

Q. Who am I with?

Q. What country am I in?

Q. What am I doing?

Q. What do I wish I could do every day?

Q. Who would I love to spend time with?

Q. If I could do any career/hobby in the world, what
would it be?

WHAT DOES MOTIVATION MEAN TO YOU?

WHAT DO YOU MOST DESIRE IN LIFE?

EXPLORING YOUR DEVELOPMENT

Q. What would you do if you were brave enough?

Q. What have you done that you never thought you would/could?

Q. Describe a spontaneous action that led to some thing incredible.

Q. What challenges are you ready to face?

Q. What would you do if you had a spare hour?

Q. What would you do if you had a spare afternoon?

Q. What would you do if you had a spare weekend?

Q. What achievements (big or small) are you most proud of?

Q. What would you like to learn if time and money was no issue?

Q. What are you good at?

Q. What would you like to improve?

Q. What causes you stress (job, finances, relation ships, health)?

Q. What does that stress feel like for you (mentally, physically, and emotionally)?

Q. How do you currently cope with stress?

Q. What strategies would you like to implement in your life to combat/deal with stress?

Q. How long do you spend online every day?

Q. How often do you use social media?

Q. If you set aside time for a social media break, what would you miss?

Q. What could you do instead if you weren't online?

Q. Who motivates you?

Q. What keeps you motivated?

Q. Who do you admire?

Q. Who do you miss?

Q. What's the best piece of advice you've ever been given?

Q. What do you treasure most in the world?

Q. What did you learn in childhood that has sustained you through life?

Q. How do you treat others?

Q. How do others treat you?

Q. How do you treat yourself?

Q. What is your proudest moment?

Q. What is your funniest memory?

Q. What is your most embarrassing moment/memory?

Q. What countries would you like to visit?

Q. What is your ideal job?

Q. What activities/hobbies would you like to try?

ACKNOWLEDGMENTS

I must start by thanking my holistic clients, blog readers, and networking connections. Without your inquisitive minds, thoughtful questions, and thirst for knowledge, I would never have pieced together this book.

Thanks also to my three children, who are my motivation and inspiration to continue doing what I do. You prove to me every day that I did the best job with the tools I had at my disposal, and I rocked it! I'm so proud of you all. I can't mention my children without shouting out to my amazing parents who support me in everything I do; they are my most devoted fans.

Thanks to everyone on the BHC Press team who help me so much. Special thanks to Vern for continuing to make me weep with joy upon every cover reveal, and to Joni for keeping me calm, focused, and fully energised.

Finally, writing is such a lonely road, and when your project is all about asking for help, embracing change, and inspiring connections then I must include a heartfelt thank you to Susan, my editorial Yoda and all-round superstar who encompasses all the above. She has guided me along this path with grace, professionalism, and humour, and long may our friendship continue.

ABOUT THE AUTHOR

Shelley Wilson is a multi-award-winning blogger and author. Her motivational and personal development blog has received numerous awards and was named a Top 10 UK Personal Development Blog. She is the author of *How I Changed My Life in a Year!*, *How I Motivated Myself to Succeed*, *Motivate Me! An Oracle Guidebook*, and *Meditation for Children*.

Shelley divides her writing time between motivational non-fiction for adults and the fantasy worlds of her young adult fiction. Her non-fiction books combine motivation and self-help with a healthy dose of humor, and her YA novels combine myth, legend and fairy tales with a side order of demonic chaos.

Shelley is an obsessive list maker who loves pizza, vampires, mythology, and history. She resides in Solihull, West Midlands, UK, where she lives with her three grown-up children and her mischievous black cat, Luna.

Connect with Shelley at:
Author Website: www.shelleywilsonauthor.com
Facebook: FantasyAuthorSLWilson
Twitter: @ShelleyWilson72
Instagram: authorslwilson
Publisher's Website: www.bhcpress.com